The Maine Birthday Book

Tonya Shevenell, author | Laura Dee Winslow, illustrator.
Copyright ©2019 Home Ice Productions - Portland, Maine
Library of Congress Control Number: 2019907347

ISBN 978-1-7339-5160-9

Published by Home Ice Productions
P.O. Box 10418
Portland, Maine 04104
www.homeiceproductions.com

Design: Peter Shevenell

Printed in China.
Second printing, 2020.

The Maine Birthday Book

By
Tonya Shevenell

Illustrated by
Laura Winslow

HOW DO YOU SAY YOUR NAME?

DEER-AGO.

HOME ICE
PRODUCTIONS

Portland, Maine

Hello!

It's my BIRTHDAY!

My friends are on their way.
They'll be here any minute!

Everything's ready!

Except *one* thing...

My birthday wish.

I don't know what to wish for.

Maybe my friends can help!

They come from all over Maine...

From forests, mountains, rivers;
ocean, islands and lakes.

I'll ask *them* for ideas!

Welcome, friends!

Henry! Doodles! Socks! You're all here!
Thank you for making this a special day!

Soon it will be time for me to make a birthday wish.

But I'm not sure what to do.
Will you help me think of a wish?

If it was your birthday,
what would you do?

What if we take turns telling you about our birthdays?

That might help you think of a special wish!

Cumberland County
White-tailed Deer

I'll go first!

Hello! My name is Fenway.
I'm from Cumberland County.

On my birthday, my firefly friends light up the whole field
with a fireworks show for me and my family!

What if you wish for
magical night lights?

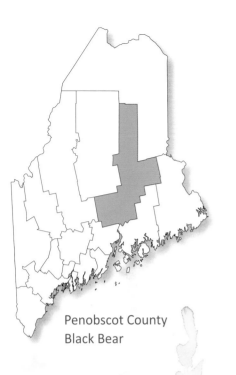

Penobscot County
Black Bear

I'll go next!

Hi! My name is Socks. I'm from Penobscot County.

I have a winter birthday, but my family **hibernates** in the winter.

That's why I have my birthday party in the summer!

We go wild blueberry picking, then we have a blueberry picnic at the lake.

My wish is for
sweet wild blueberries
every day of the year.

Wild blueberries are a purr-fect snack.

Hi, all! My name's Pilot. My home is in Sagadahoc County.

On my birthday, my friends and I play NASA cats!
We fly missions to our favorite planets! We will discover
if there are mice on Mars.

My wish is to be the best spaceship builder in the world...

...and the inventor of a cat constellation in the sky.

Sagadahoc County
Maine Coon Cat

An inventor! I'm named after an inventor!

Chester, that is... Chester Greenwood, from Franklin County!

He invented lots of things, but he's famous for earmuffs.

My birthday's in the summer, but I invented a half-birthday party
in the winter, so we can wear our earmuffs!

We go

    sliding...

        skiing...

           skating!

We love snow!

Franklin County
Snowshoe Hare

I wish for LOTS OF IT.

We get lots of snow where I live!

I'm Crosby and I'm from Maine's BIGGEST county, Aroostook.
We have a BIG neighbor too: CANADA.

My friends from Maine and Canada explore streams
and ponds with me on my birthday.

We love cold water, tall tales and tellin' fish stories.

My wish? **More fish!**

Aroostook County
Brook Trout

It's fun having
lots of friends
in the neighborhood!

Oxford County
Dragonfly

That sounds like us! I'm Shavey. I'm Maevy!
We're from the western part of Maine, in Oxford County.

On our birthday, we fly to New Hampshire and jam
with our friends in the Granite State. We sing and
dance and play, then we hum the whole way home!

Dirigo, you know those days when you're feelin' the music...

What could be better!

Sweet solos and **soaring** harmonies!

That is our wish for you.

Androscoggin County
Beaver

Shavey and Maevy, I live down river from you
in Androscoggin County. My name is Sawyer.

I get up and get busy on my birthday!

My grandparents taught me to start the day doing something
kind for someone else. I invite my friends to help.

When we finish, we feel really good.

My grandparents call that **the Birthday Bonus!**

My wish is for everyone
to feel the Birthday Bonus.

Somerset County
Fisher

Hi. My name's Shade. I am a fisher from Somerset County.

But I do not fish. I climb trees.

My friends don't fish either. They climb trees.

None of us fishers fish—ever—and definitely not on our birthdays.

On our birthdays...we climb trees.

Not just any trees. Our **favorite, special, party** trees.

And we tell tall tales. That's what fishers do.

My wish is to tell the **tallest** tall tale, in the tallest tree of all!

Lincoln County
Alewife

Hello!
My name's Flash.

I live in Lincoln County — but part of the year, I live at sea.

I swim from salt water to fresh water;
from the Atlantic Ocean to rivers,
    lakes,
      streams
        and ponds.
          I'm on the Run!

It's nice to be in one place.
And *reeeee-lax*.

I hula-hoop on my
birthday, and watch the
town parade go by.

I wish the whole world would hula-hoop together.

Flash, you live near me, when you're not out to sea.
My name is Milton. I'm from Kennebec County.

Here's my birthday idea: **PLAY GAMES!**
Sports games, card games, board games!
You can even make up your **own** games!

We have so much fun, I always wish
we could play *ONE MORE!*

Kennebec County
Gray Squirrel

Hancock County
Lobster

Ahoy, Mateys! As you can see...

I'm into yoga!

My friends and I spread out on the ocean floor and make poses.
We invent funny names for them: like the Unfurling Birthday Twirling
and the Double-Bubble-Party Pose!

Sometimes we make the downward-facing ducks laugh.

My wish is for F L E X I B I L I T Y.

Oh! Almost forgot!

My name is Cadillac —
and I live in the coastal waters
of Hancock County.

under water
YOGA

Piscataquis County
Moose

I'll try yoga. Maybe in the
mornings at the moose bog!

Hello, I'm Henry.
I live in Piscataquis County,
near Moosehead Lake.

My birthday is in the spring
during fiddlehead season.

We canoe to our favorite
fiddlehead picking spot.

I can't tell you where it is...
because it's a secret!

My wish is for a best
friend you can tell
your secrets to.

Yippeeeee...it's my turn!

Hello, I'm Doodles! Most of the year I live at sea, but when I'm home in Maine, I live on an island in Knox County.

On my birthday, I go island-hopping with my friends!

We climb rocks, look at our reflections in tidal pools, play on the beach and draw in the sand.

My wish is to be an artist!

Knox County
Atlantic Puffin

York County
Snowy Owl

Have you ever drawn a lighthouse? Or an owl?
Our heads swivel around kind of like a lighthouse!

I love lOOking at lighthouses with my big yellow eyes.

My name is Nicholas. I don't live in Maine, but I fly south
from Canada to York County in the winter
for the great views.

Great food, too!

My wish is to see
others, and be seen,
as one-of-a-kind,
original
and
unique...

...like a snowflake.

Or a lighthouse!

Or a coyote like me!
Hello, I'm Sydney. I live in Waldo County.

When winter turns to spring, and the snow has melted away
iiiiiiit's magical **MUD** season!

The birds sing louder,
the sun shines warmer,
the earth smells earthier,
and baby buds pop like
big bloomin' surprises...

THAT'S WHEN IT'S
MY BIRTHDAY!

Waldo County
Coyote

To celebrate, I hike with my family. We *hoowwwl* along the way!

I wish for happy trails and a **spring** in your step.

1 MILE

HARBOR

The Wabanaki Tribes of Maine

Micmac

Maliseet

Penobscot

Passamaquoddy Loon

I step, fly, and swim!
Hello, my name is Molly. In the summer
I live on lakes on Passamaquoddy land.

Maybe you've heard me making maps
with my voice? My songs are signals,
so my friends know where I am.

That's the call
of the loon.

Our birthdays are
special concert
events...

Every loon
in the lake
has a part!

My wish is for
everyone to carry a song
in their heart.

Washington County
Bald Eagle

I hear your songs, Molly.

I'm Addison, and I live in Washington County,
the easternmost part of Maine.

My family's birthday tradition is to share the stories of our names and birth.

We honor the beginnings of each other
like we honor the beginning
of each day at first light.

My wish is for sunrises that make you feel like **every day** is your birthday.

Do you know the story of your name, Dirigo?

I do!

Dirigo means "I lead."

I lead by my *chickadee-dee-dee* call
and by listening to what other
chickadees sing back.

Dirigo is Maine's motto!

It's on the state flag.

The North Star is a symbol
of the motto...and my name.

When I look in the sky at night,
the North Star makes me feel at
home, wherever I am.

Star-gazing and making wishes
are some of my favorite things to do.
Especially on my birthday...

...with all of you!

It's time to make my birthday wish!
Thanks to you, I know exactly what to do!

Now—will you
help me count
down?

Yes! 5-4-3-2-1...

HAPPY

BIRTHDAY!

What will you do on YOUR birthday?

Dear Journal,

What a day! I was crawling along the dandelion trail when a moose came around the corner with a beaver on his head. They were going to a birthday party and invited me to tag along!

At the party, I made new friends. They told me stories.

Milton the squirrel is named after a boy from Maine, born way back in 1836, who made up games that people still play today! His name was Milton Bradley.

Cadillac the lobster is named for a mountain so tall, it's one of the first things the sun sees when it rises over Maine!

There were so many stories, I wrote them in my special journal so I won't forget. You know what? Stories are all around us!

Sometimes they're hidden and you have to look and listen for them.

Sometimes they need your imagination to help them out.

Stories are like friends that
want to be with you, no matter
your age or stage, or whether
you walk, swim, crawl or fly.

Well, Journal... that's my story
for today!

Onward! (and upward!)

PS - I made a wish, too!
Can you guess what it is?

MALIBU MAINE
Home of the
stories Journal
www.Malibumaine.com